The Crystal Set Kid

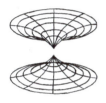  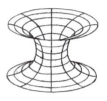

Roger Carr

Illustrated by Chris Lynch

KINGSCOURT / McGRAW-HILL

The Crystal Set Kid
Copyright © 2001 Rigby Heinemann

Rigby is part of Harcourt Education, a division of
Reed International Books Australia Pty Ltd ABN 70 001 002 357.

Text by Roger Carr
Illustrations by Chris Lynch

Designed by Andrew Cunningham

KINGSCOURT/McGRAW-HILL

Shoppenhangers Road, Maidenhead
Berkshire, SL6 2QL
Telephone: 01628 502730
Fax: 01628 635895

www.kingscourt.co.uk
E-mail: enquiries@kingscourt.co.uk

Printed in Australia by Advance Press

10 9 8 7 6 5 4 3 2 1

ISBN: 0-07-710325-4

Contents

CHAPTER ONE

The Crystal

"HE'S GOING INVISIBLE!" Charlie cried in horror.

Charlie and Mim were looking from the window of Darren's bedroom. Darren was standing on the back lawn, shouting. But his voice was fading, and his body seemed to be disappearing.

"Can you turn it off..." Darren's voice called faintly.

Mim turned back to the desk. She looked over the wires, the coil and earpiece.

"It hasn't got a switch," she shouted angrily. "Stupid thing!"

1

"He's nearly invisible," Charlie said in horror. "He's disappearing."

It had all begun two weeks ago on a class excursion. Mr Johns had hired a bus to take the geography class to an area where they could explore the bed of an old stream.

They had taken notebooks, some of the school's instant cameras, some garden trowels, and lunch. No-one had forgotten their lunch, but quite a few had forgotten their notebooks.

"You don't get out of it that easily," Mr Johns had said. "I've brought plenty of spare notebooks and pencils." But when lunch time came, he found he had forgotten to bring his own lunch.

Darren Miller always remembered everything. He dug in the sand of the old stream bed like a dog looking for a favourite bone he had buried somewhere. When it was his turn for one of the cameras, he photographed everything he found. When he did not have the camera, he made sketches and notes.

He was that sort of kid. He was interested in lots of things and whatever he did, he did it really well. He was about middle height in the class, with short sandy hair and freckled skin. He looked as if he should be a real nerd, but he wasn't. He never tried to show how smart he was, or tell anyone anything. He just enjoyed doing stuff and did it.

Miriam Sexton, Mim for short, wasn't like Darren. She always spoke her mind and she had a bad temper. But Mim and Darren were good friends, even though they had quite different personalities. Charlie Andrews was their friend, too. He was always quiet, but so stubborn and strong that he nearly always got his own way.

"The three strangers," Mr Johns called them. They were not alike in any way but they were always together.

At lunch time, the three of them shared the food they had brought with Mr Johns. Darren gave him his boiled egg.

Mim let him have the first drink from her bottle of cola. Charlie gave him a plastic container of curry. Mr Johns only ate a small amount of the curry, though, before he had to quickly ask Mim for another drink.

"That curry is delicious," Mr Johns said to Charlie when he had cooled his mouth down.

"Yes, it is," Charlie said. "My mum often makes it."

Suddenly, they heard shouting.

"Mr Johns! Mr Johns!" Bella cried. "I've found diamonds! A whole heap of them!"

Everyone scrambled to where Bella was digging. The hole was small, and not very deep, but her whole trowel was filled with small, glittering crystals about the size and shape of peas.

Everyone said *wow* and *gee* and *you're rich* and wished they had been the ones to make the find.

"There are heaps more," Bella said as she tipped the ones in the trowel onto the sand. She dug a new lot from the hole.

Mr Johns put three of them in the palm of his hand, and then rolled them around.

Sharp reflections came from the glittering crystals as he moved them.

"I didn't know you could get diamonds this easily," Miska said.

"I don't think you can," Mr Johns said. "I don't think they are diamonds."

Everyone was disappointed.

"What do you think they are, then?" Josh asked.

Mr Johns shook his head. "I don't know," he said. He looked into the hole Bella had dug. "Are there any more?"

Bella tipped the second lot onto the sand, and used the trowel to dig around in the bottom of the hole. She could only find another five.

"I thought there were heaps," she said.

"They might have come in a meteorite," Jim said. "Yeeeeow... pow!"

"That's certainly possible," Mr Johns agreed. "If Bella says it's okay, I think you should all take one home and see if you can find out what they are."

"Sure," Bella agreed.

"We'll make it a part of the excursion project," Mr Johns said. "It'll be interesting.

Maybe someone has found something like this around here before. Use the school library and your local library."

"And the Internet!" Darren finished.

Darren frequently used the Internet at home. But no matter how many sites he searched with the word crystal in them, he could not find any that described the little pea-sized crystals Bella had found.

Something that did come up in his searches was "crystal set". It came up so often, he decided to see what it was.

One of the websites described it as the first kind of radio set ever built. It gave instructions on how to build one. It looked so simple, Darren decided to try—and it worked!

It did not even need a battery, and he could listen to three local radio stations through the earpiece he attached to it.

"Why do they call it a crystal set?" Charlie asked when he first saw it.

"Because it needs a crystal to make it work," Darren explained. He pointed to the piece of crystal he had bought to make the set. "It's a piece of pyrites. You can buy other stuff to do the same thing, now, but in the old days you had to have a crystal."

"Why don't you try one of the crystals that Bella found on the excursion," Mim suggested. "Just to see what happens?"

"Yeah!" Darren said. "I wonder what would happen?"

"Well, don't just wonder!" Mim snapped. "Try it!"

"Don't be angry, Mim," Charlie said softly. But she ignored him.

Darren got the pea-sized crystal from the plastic box he kept it in beside the computer. He loosened the tiny metal claws that kept the pyrites in place, and tightened them again on the new crystal. Then he put the earpiece in and slowly turned the dial.

"Well?" Mim demanded.

"Shh! I'm trying to listen."

The sound he heard was like tumbling waves, the same as it was when he used the pyrites in the crystal set. He turned the dial, but that didn't make any difference at all.

That was odd. Turning the dial when the other crystal was in, made the sound keep changing until he could hear a station.

Darren took the earpiece out. "It's sort of working," he said. "I'm going to check the aerial. You two can listen, if you like."

The aerial was a long piece of wire. Crystal sets needed long aerials. Darren and his father had put it up. It ran from the roof of their house, across the back lawn, to a tree on the edge of the hospital car park next door.

Darren stood on the lawn and looked up at the wire. It was the same as it had always been. He looked across to his bedroom window. He could see Mim had the earpiece in, and Charlie was watching her.

"Has it changed?" he called.

Mim shook her head.

"That crystal's not going to work then," he called back. He was disappointed. He had thought it might bring in some different radio stations or something. He tried to turn to go back inside but his legs wouldn't work. They suddenly felt very weak and just would not move.

"Huh?" he said aloud, and tried to bend

down to feel them. But his back would not bend. He went to feel his back with one hand. But his arms were not working…

He looked back to his window, and was suddenly very frightened. The whole house seemed to be fading away. The trees were fading away, too. And the fences…

"Help!" he shouted, except it was not a real shout. It was more like a whisper.

The crystal. It was something to do with the crystal Bella had found. It was sending something through the aerial that was making everything invisible.

He sucked in as much air as he could, and used all his strength to cry out, "Turn it off… !"

Mim reached him first. "What's happening?" she shouted angrily. "What are you doing?

And you didn't even put a switch on the stupid thing."

He tried to tell her to keep away. Tried to tell her to go back inside and just pull one of the wires off. Any wire. But he could not speak now.

Charlie reached them then. He dashed out onto the lawn and grabbed them each by one arm and tried to pull them off the lawn. They were almost invisible. He was frightened his hands might go right through them. But they were solid, and when he pulled

them back, they began to come with him. Then he began to feel weak, too. He could not pull them more than a step.

"What's happening?" Charlie whispered.

The almost invisible shapes of the other two just stared at him.

"Are we dying?" Charlie asked.

Still they did not answer.

He kept his grip on their arms. They still felt solid while everything around faded slowly away. The house, the trees, the fences, the lawn faded until there was nothing but white light everywhere with only the dim figures of Mim and Darren visible.

Keep holding on, Charlie told himself. I mustn't let go. He could feel their arms in his hands. But he could not tighten his hands, and he could not let go, either.

He looked down. Even the lawn under his feet was gone. He was standing on nothing, yet he did not seem to be falling. It was more like floating. No, it was not even like that. If he had been floating, he would have been moving, if only a little bit...

At least he could move his eyes. Charlie and Mim could, too. They were looking down as he had done. Then across to him and to each other.

We must be dead, Charlie thought. We must have got some kind of electric shock from the aerial and been killed. But I wouldn't be able to think. And I wouldn't be able to see, if I was dead. If only we could speak to each other, he thought. Charlie was glad he had snatched their arms. It kept them all together.

"Faster than light," a voice said.

Both Mim and Charlie flashed their eyes to Darren's face.

"Faster than light," the voice said again. It was Darren speaking.

"I can hear you!" Mim cried.

"So can I!" Charlie said. "I can see you better, too. And I can move my hands."

"Don't let go!" Darren said. "We have to stay together."

"Why?" Mim demanded. "Why do we have to stay together? We're dead! Your stupid crystal set electrocuted us."

"No, it didn't," Darren protested, quickly. "A crystal set hasn't got any electricity. It wasn't connected to anything."

"Except the aerial," Mim said. "That was probably across the power lines."

"It was not!" Darren retorted. "Dad and I were very careful when we put it up. It didn't go across anything. And, anyway, none of us even touched the aerial."

"Why can we talk now?" Charlie asked. "Why can I move my hands? Why can I see you clearly?"

"I don't know," Darren admitted. "I don't understand what's happening."

"Well, you should. It's your stupid crystal set," Mim said. "You made it and you showed it to us."

"But it was your idea to try the crystal we found on the excursion," Charlie told her. "I think it was the crystal that did this."

"If that crystal did come in a meteorite, it means it came from outer space," Darren said. "I wonder, could it have somehow sent us into space…?"

"No!" Mim shouted. "I am not going into outer space!" She jerked her arm free from Charlie's hand and began trying to pound on the whiteness that surrounded them. "Let me out! Let me out!" she kept shouting angrily.

"If you don't let me out right now then I'm going... I'm going to... to do something!"

It was almost as if Mim's shouting had worked. Suddenly, they were standing on grass again, and the whiteness all around them was flowing away.

"Thank you!" Mim shouted. But she had said thank you too soon.

"This isn't my lawn," Darren said as the world around them became clearer. "I don't know where we are."

CHAPTER TWO

Phone Home

I T WAS A HUGE LAWN, well kept. But it was not a back garden. It seemed to be part of a park. They were standing near a fountain.

"You don't have a fountain in your back yard!" Mim snapped at Darren, as though he was trying to trick her. "This is not your lawn at all!"

"Something very strange has happened," Charlie said.

Mim snorted. It made her sound like a horse. "Nothing strange has happened," she said. "I'm just in a stupid dream with you two and I'm not staying!"

"Mim! Where are you going?" Darren shouted. "Come back!"

"I'm walking out of this dream," Mim called back without turning. "I always walk out of bad dreams!"

"It's not a dream!" Darren called after her. "Charlie's here. I'm here. We can't all be dreaming the same thing." He began kicking at the lawn with the heel of one shoe. "Help, Charlie. We'll have to go after her. But I don't want to go until I've marked the exact place we landed."

"What do you mean, landed?" Charlie asked as he began kicking another mark to cross Darren's line.

"Well ... whatever we did," Darren said. "That will do. We'll be able to find that again. Just remember it was near the fountain. Come on."

They ran across the grass after Mim. Darren looked around as he ran. To their left and their right and behind them, the grass ended in dense shrubbery. Ahead of them, across the street from Mim, there were shops.

"Why don't you leave me alone?" Mim

demanded when they fell in beside her. "I'm getting out of this dream."

"You wish," Darren said. "Why isn't the traffic making any noise?" They turned and hurried along the street towards a set of traffic lights. "I'd think I was deaf, except I can hear your voices and the sound of our feet."

"All the cars look so modern," Charlie said as they stopped at the lights. "I think they're all electric."

"Why are people in the cars pointing at us?" Mim demanded. "We're not weird or anything."

"I think we might be, to them," Darren said.

"Look how they're all dressed. And there's something different about them. They've got sort of longer heads than we have. And they're a bit thinner, too."

"And their skin," Charlie said. "It's sort of bluey-grey."

"They look as if they're all going to some fancy dress party," Mim said. "But it's only the middle of the afternoon."

"I think it's about the middle of the next century," Darren replied, as the lights changed and they walked across the street. "I think we're in the future. I wonder where we could find today's date?" He stepped towards a passing shopper. "Excuse me. Can you tell me the date?"

The guy glanced at his watch—which was probably a telephone and computer as well, Darren guessed. "Fifteenth of August," the guy said without stopping.

"I mean the year," Darren said, following him along the street.

"Yeah… yeah, whatever," the guy said without even glancing back.

Darren shrugged and went back to the others. He felt too silly to try asking anyone else who was walking by. But he had to find out what year they were in.

"We need a telephone," Mim said. "I told my mother I'd only be round at your place for half-an-hour. Not a hundred years."

"Don't joke about it!" Charlie said; and for the first time Mim realised the boys were serious; that this might not be a dream.

"Then we have to find a telephone, fast," Mim said. "We seriously have to!"

They looked up and down the street, then Mim chose a direction and the boys followed her. They paused each time she stopped someone to ask for a telephone; then moved on as each person she asked stepped quickly around her—as though she was some kind of danger to them. But she kept trying, her voice impatient, until a tall, thin young man, who seemed rather nervous, stopped.

"Telephone?" he asked. He blinked several times and rubbed his short black hair nervously. "Telephone? Um…you mean a cellcom."

"Well, a cellcom," Mim said impatiently. "Do you know where I can find one?"

"Oh, yes, certainly," the young man said.

"Can you tell me what the date is?" Darren asked.

Mim interrupted. "I just want a tele—er, cellcom. I've got to ring my mother!"

"I'll… I'll help you find one," the young man said, looking vaguely up and down the street, then beginning to walk.

Darren shrugged to Charlie, and they fell in with Mim and the young man.

A few minutes later, the young man stopped and pointed into a brightly lit area between two stores. "In there," he said to Mim, then turned back to Darren. "It's August the fifteenth, 2120."

Mim came bursting back out of the cellcom, furious. "The stupid thing won't take my pre-paid card! And it won't take money! How am I going to make a phone call now?"

The young man felt through his pockets and pulled out a handful of coins and tokens, He sorted through them. "Um, use these," he said, giving half-a-dozen tokens to Mim.

Mim got out some money, but the young

man shook his head. "They're... um, not worth much. Don't worry about it."

"Oh... thanks!" Mim said and she disappeared back into the cellcom.

Darren and Charlie wanted to follow, but they did not like to simply walk away when the young man had been so helpful. He did not appear to want to leave them, either.

"Um, you're new here?" the young man asked, then put out his hand. "I'm Mitch. Mitch Lukin. I do maths."

They shook hands with him, and introduced themselves.

"I think we might have come from there," Darren said. He pointed to the park across the street. "We don't remember that park, though."

Mitch turned and studied the park as though he had just noticed it. "Um, I've seen old maps..."

"There should be houses there and a big hospital," Darren said.

Mitch blinked several times, surprised. "Um... hospital? I think there was one there, on, um... very old maps."

Darren felt goosebumps all over him.

"A hospital? Over there?" he asked, pointing. "A hospital?" he repeated.

"I ... um, think so," Mitch said.

"Then we were still in my back yard," Darren whispered, almost to himself. "We didn't move anywhere ... "

"Except a hundred and something years," Charlie said.

Mitch was suddenly excited. "You're saying ... " he began.

"Come and help me!" Mim shouted. "The stupid thing says it's not a number. I know it's a number. I've used it a million times!"

That embarrassed Mitch, and he waved towards Mim in an apologetic kind of way. "Yes, um ... go and help her. I've taken up too much of your time."

"Well, thanks for the tokens," Charlie said, as he turned to go in to help Mim.

"And how to find the cellcom," Darren said, following Charlie in. "What do you mean, they say it's not a number?" he asked Mim.

"I mean, they say it's not a number!" Mim shouted at him.

"I'll try mine," Darren said, following her to the keypad. At least that looked familiar.

While they tried, Charlie found the directory screen, and worked out how to use it.

"They said the same thing," Darren said, replacing the phone.

"There are three extra digits now," Charlie said. "I've looked up my name. There's a heap of them. But not my parents."

Mim and Darren almost jumped across to Charlie's screen.

"Brilliant!" Mim said. "Look up 'Sexton' and I'll recognise a street or something."

But she didn't; so he looked up "Miller" and found about ten thousand.

"Hey, that's me!" Darren shouted suddenly, stabbing at the screen. "Ouch!" He'd been so excited, he hurt his finger. "Look! Darren 'Dusty' Miller! That has to be someone I know. 'Dusty' is the family nickname. Key it in for me, will you?" He shook his hand again. "That was my working finger that I hurt."

Mim put in the number, and handed the phone to Darren.

"This is a pre-paid message," a voice said, and then another voice spoke. It was a male voice, and it sounded old. Darren made urgent signals to the other two to come close and listen.

"Don't try and get in touch again, young Darren. This is a pre-paid message that has no trace, and will simply be repeated twenty times before being erased. I remember how helpless I felt when I was making this call. Don't be afraid. Just go along with whatever happens and you will not be disappointed. I will be dead many, many years when you hear this message. Crystal sets, huh."

Darren let the phone bounce down into its cradle, his mouth slightly open, his eyes just staring ahead.

"Huh?" Mim exclaimed.

Darren shook his head, not yet able to speak.

"Who was it?" Charlie asked.

Darren swallowed. "It was me," he squeaked. "Let's get something to eat and try and work this out."

Charlie and Mim looked at each other, still confused by the telephone message. Then they went after Darren. He was already turning into another shop along the street, and they ran to catch up with him. The way people were staring at them, they wished Mitch was back. At least he didn't act like they weren't normal.

Darren was already coming out of the takeaway he had found when they arrived.

"There's a policeman watching us," Mim whispered. "Behind us. He doesn't look friendly."

Neither of the boys heard her.

"Everything costs heaps!" Darren said. "I've only got a few pounds." He held up some coins. "And, anyway, everything is being sold for worldmarks, whatever they are."

"They must take real money, too," Mim said, hunger making her forget about the policeman.

"Well, I think we should pool our money and save as much as we can," Darren said. "We don't know how long it will be before … well, anything."

"Okay, one loaf of bread," Charlie said.

"That will be cheap, and will feed us until morning. Let's find a bread shop."

"I've got a whole proper dinner waiting for me at home," Mim complained. But the others took no notice. Charlie led them into a bakery and pointed to a large loaf of white bread.

The woman behind the counter tried hard not to stare at the three odd-looking children. She put her wrap-wand over the loaf, then took it down from the shelf as the spring-wrap cellulose enclosed it.

"Four-twenty," she said.

Charlie turned to the others, making motions with his hand for them to give him their coins, then handed some to the woman.

"What are they?" she asked, pulling back.

"For the loaf of bread," Charlie said.

A man had been watching them closely. He came forward now and looked at the money in Charlie's hand.

"That's not money," the woman said.

"It is, actually," the man said. "It's very old, though. Where did you find it?" he asked Charlie.

"We just had it," Charlie said, then

became quite upset at the thought of having nothing to eat. "We really need that bread."

"I don't know what your money is worth to a collector," the man said. He took out a wallet. "Here. I'll give you fifty worldmarks for it. I don't think I'm cheating you."

"It doesn't matter if you are," Charlie said, handing the money over and taking the fifty worldmarks from the man. "Thanks." He handed the woman five worldmarks.

"Come on!" Mim snapped. "I'm really starving!"

Charlie took the change, gave the man a quick smile, and led the way out of the shop.

"Let's go over to the park and eat it," Darren said. "Everyone's staring at us too much. I feel like someone's going to do something to us."

They went back to the crossing. Night was coming down quickly, and the shops and traffic were lighting up. That was normal.

But there was still no noise, and that made everything seem strange.

"What are you talking about? Who's going to do something?" Mim demanded while they waited at the lights. She looked behind. "That cop's gone, now. Anyway, we haven't done anything wrong."

"We're just too different to be safe," Darren said. He led the way across the street, then began to run. "Down to the shrubbery," he said.

They pushed in among the shrubs and found a place to sit. Charlie broke the loaf into three pieces and they ate hungrily.

"We should have bought two loaves," Mim complained as the last of their bread disappeared.

"We don't know how long this money has to last," Charlie said. "That was enough for dinner."

"Dinner! That was just a snack," Mim cried. "Aren't you going to get us back home tonight?" she demanded of Darren.

"Me?" Darren asked in surprise. "I didn't bring us."

"We should go to the police," Mim said.

"I should have gone back when I saw that one looking at us."

"We don't need police," Darren said. "We need a professor. A whole heap of them."

"Then we should go to a university," Charlie said.

Mim stood up. "Come on, then."

"As soon as it's light tomorrow morning," Darren said.

"That's too late!" Mim shouted at him.

"Now's too late," Charlie said, pointing through the shrubs.

Across the grass, in their direction, came two dark figures. There were bright flashes of light coming from some kind of badge on their coats as they walked.

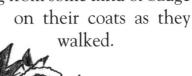

"Quick!" Darren hissed, scrambling to his feet and pushing urgently through the bushes in the opposite direction to the approaching figures.

But when he got to the other side of the shrubbery, there was a net and two more of the dark figures.

CHAPTER THREE

Ferals

ONE OF THE OFFICERS shone a bright light on the three wrapped in the net. "Ferals," he said. "I've heard there are one or two tribes of them in the hill country."

"We are not feral anything!" Mim screamed, thrashing about in the net. But thrashing about did nothing. The net was light and fine and it seemed to stick to them with some kind of static electricity. The more she struggled, the tighter it gripped. It just exhausted her.

"We're not going to try and get away," Charlie called.

"We need help," Darren said.

"Let me out!" Mim screamed, but she was not thrashing around, now.

There was the snap and swishing of branches from the shrubbery, and the two officers who had approached across the grass stepped out.

"Nice one," the first one said when he saw the catch. "Should we stun them?"

"We're not trying to get away!" Darren said again quickly. "We just need help."

"I don't fancy getting bitten," one of the officers said.

"We don't bite!" Darren shouted. "We're not animals, we're human beings like you!"

"Why don't you tell us all about it," said the first one again.

"We're lost in time," Darren said. "We were standing on the lawn in my back yard in the year 2000 when... when I don't know what happened. We need help to get back."

"Good story," the officer said. "Maybe we just leave them netted. Should be able to lift this little lot."

"You bite once," the other warned, "and

you're out!" He bent and gave the net between Darren and Charlie a quick twist. It left Darren in a net of his own. Then he did the same between Charlie and Mim.

One of them picked Mim up and heaved her onto his shoulder. "Notice the skin colours?" he said as he walked. "All different and one of them's spotted."

"I'm not spotted!" Darren protested, but they ignored him, and just kept talking.

"You can always tell a feral that way, although I hear they are usually in tribes of the one skin colour."

"Seems odd when you think about it. That we were all different colours once," said the one carrying Charlie.

"Yeah. I wonder what it was like when everyone was different, like these kids are," another said.

The officers carried their prisoners across to a van. One of them opened the back door and they bundled the children inside.

It was when the door hissed closed, and Charlie found some force was locking the net so tightly to the floor that he could not move even a finger, that he began to cry. For the first time, he felt helpless, and realised just how much trouble they were in. Crying seemed useless, but he could not stop.

Then Mim heard him, and began to cry, too. But Mim did not do it quietly. She never did anything quietly. Mim sobbed and howled and called for her mother and father.

Darren did not notice. He was thinking about the way they had been locked to the floor. The nets had seemed amazing enough, but the force that was acting like seat restraints seemed even more so. If nets were not needed as well, it would be a good way to protect people against accidents. Better than seat belts. He must remember that when he left school—if he ever went back—and try to invent it.

The van braked, then the door opened and they were lifted out. Charlie was still crying, but soundlessly, while Mim really howled as they were carried into a building and dumped on a hard, shiny floor in something that seemed like a large fish tank. As each of them was put down, the net was taken off, but they were so stiff they could hardly move.

Mim changed her howling for cries of pain as she tried to make her limbs work. She wanted the officers to know how much she was suffering.

The boys had the same problem, but kept silent. The new situation was enough for Charlie to regain control, and stop crying.

Darren could not keep his eyes still. They were in a very, very large room. There were several fish tanks, the same as the one they were in, aligned down the centre of the room. They were not attached to each other. A couple of them had people inside them. Prisoners, he guessed.
Like them.

Three young police officers came over to their tank and stared at them. When Mim saw them, she stopped her noisy howling.

She glared at them and poked out her tongue.

"That will really help," Darren said. "Now they'll think we're half-wits as well as ferals." His limbs were less stiff, now, and he got painfully to his knees. "We're supposed to be impressing them as intelligent people. Not zoo specimens."

Mim snapped her mouth shut, and continued to glare at the three officers. It seemed to amuse them, and they went off, laughing.

Slowly, all three were recovering. Charlie got to his knees and reached out and tapped on the wall, just to be sure it was there. It was solid. He moved back and sat in the centre. The other two moved close to him. All three sat, staring out.

"I wonder why they chose such an urky grey colour for their skin?" Mim said, her voice normal now, as though she had not been weeping and wailing so loudly only a moment before.

"Everything you do is an act," Darren said crossly.

"I know!" Charlie said suddenly.

"Know what?" Mim demanded.

"How they got that skin colour," Charlie

said. "It always happened when I was in preschool!"

"What did?" Mim demanded.

"We had sticks of coloured clay for making stuff. When it was new, there was red, black, yellow, green, blue, white—a whole heap of colours. But after we'd played with it for a while, and mushed it up a few times, the only colour left was," Charlie pointed at the people watching them, "that odd bluey-grey colour!"

"Everyone in the world must have got mixed in!" Darren said, then became glum. "I wish they were just clay people. They're going to lock us up and—"

"Put us on show," Mim said.

"Well, something," Darren continued. "Whatever they do, we won't have a chance to try and get back."

"I wonder, do they know we're gone?" Charlie said. "Our mums and dads?"

"They could send a rescue mission!"

"Send it where, Mim?" asked Darren. "They'll search the city. They'll probably even search the city dump. But they won't search through time. They don't even know about it.

Wormholes are in maths books. Time travel is just in science fiction stories. Even these people don't know about it. Not the ones we've spoken to, anyway."

"Shh!" Charlie warned. "They're coming.

A man and a woman in uniform, seated behind a desk, slid into the fish tank, desk and all. They seemed to be able to move through the glass, or whatever it was, without problems.

"Turn out your pockets," the man said.

There wasn't much. Charlie had the forty-five worldmarks and change, a chewing gum wrapper and a plastic spoon.

Darren had a small notebook, a ballpoint, and the wrapper from the bread. Mim had three handkerchiefs and a pocket knife.

"And where did you say you're from?" the man asked, looking through the worldmarks.

"From the past," Darren said. "From the year 2000!"

"And you're carrying coins dated 2110 and 2115?"

"A man gave them to us," Charlie said.

"Someone is going to give a bunch of ferals a handful of worldmarks?"

"He bought the money we had," Charlie explained.

"I'll believe that when I believe time travel," the man said.

"We didn't believe it," Darren said. "We weren't even trying to time travel. It just happened, and now we want to go back."

"Why not admit you're ferals, tell us your tribe, and we'll send you back to them?" the woman asked, ignoring Darren's plea.

"Our instructions are to send you back if you carry no weapons and have no hostile intentions."

"We don't!" the three shouted together.

"We have established that, already," the woman snapped. "Otherwise you would already be dead."

"You wouldn't just…?" Charlie couldn't finish the question. He found it impossible to believe anyone would kill children.

"We would. We do," the woman said. "History has taught us such weaknesses are dangerous to a civilisation."

"So tell us which tribe you belong to, and we'll send you back," the man said. "You can be back with your own people first thing tomorrow."

"We are not ferals!" Mim shouted.

The man sighed, and turned to the woman. "Seek a banish order?" he asked.

She nodded. "Well, they certainly can't be released."

CHAPTER FOUR

Abandoned

M IM LOOKED ABOUT through half-closed eyes. She knew she was dreaming again. The bare walls, the TV, wash basin and toilet were not familiar. She closed her eyes and rolled over feeling about for Teddy. She was tired of all these bad dreams.

Then her fingers jabbed into another wall, and her eyes sprang open. She did not have a wall beside her bed. She did not have a wash basin and a toilet in her room!

She screeched loudly, and threw off the blanket. The boys heard her from the next cell where they had been put for the night.

"Mim," Charlie called. "We've been trying to get you to wake up for ages."

"I don't want to wake up," Mim cried.

But she had no choice. A police officer was already opening her cell door.

Immediately after he had left them the evening before, Mitch went to the university library. He had checked the old maps and he was right. There had been a hospital in the park. Nearly a hundred years ago.

Of course, the kids could have seen the maps. But somehow, they had not appeared to be the kind of kids who would try to hoax anyone. They were too upset, too urgent, too out of this world.

Thinking about it kept him awake most of the night, and in the morning, he drove in to Central Clearing and asked about them.

"I do maths," Mitch explained. "Have you got three feral children in here? Two boys and a girl? I was talking to them last night."

"Sorry, pal," the officer at the desk said. "The court had those ferals shipped out on a banish order half-an-hour ago."

"Come back. Please come back! I don't want to be a slave!" Mim screeched. She shook both closed fists at the small skyslip, an egg-shaped rocket with no wings, as it sped back into the air. And then she began to sob. "Please. Please come back."

The boys turned away from her. It would be too easy to join her useless pleading. They were standing in a limit-less desert of white sand. They had seen it from the windows of the skyslip, and could guess just how far it was from where they stood to the first sign of grass and trees. Probably a month's walking. But who could walk for a month without food or water? Who could walk that far, even *with* food and water, in this searing heat?

It was still morning, but already the sand burned hot through the soles of their shoes.

"Come on," Charlie said abruptly. "We'll die out here in the sun."

He began to walk towards the half-dozen spindly palms, five or so minutes away, and Darren followed.

"Don't go there!" Mim screamed from behind them. "That's where they take slaves from!"

The boys ignored her, and she ran to catch them.

"You heard what those policemen said!" she cried. "If the nomads come through, they might take us as slaves!"

Charlie stopped and turned to her. He was so angry, he bumped into Darren, who was walking with his eyes down, pushing him out of the way.

"They don't just take you from under the palms," Charlie shouted. "If they want you, they take you from wherever they find you. Don't you understand what that policeman meant? He said they might take you as slaves. If you're lucky!"

He looked so furious that Mim stopped, then stepped back. She had never seen him angry before.

"But I don't want to be a slave," she whimpered.

Charlie turned and walked after Darren, and Mim fell in behind.

The shade from the palms of the oasis felt almost cold for the first few moments. Then the heat radiating from the sands overcame it. Mim and Darren sat with their backs against a trunk, and closed their eyes against the glare.

Charlie put down the small container of food one of the policemen had given them. He walked to the well and peered in. It was black and dark. He could not see any water. But there was a crude windlass across the top, and a metal bucket standing on the other side of the well.

The handle of the bucket was tied to the rope from the windlass. Charlie put the bucket into the well, and turned the handle of the windlass to let it down.

It was an age before the rope went slack, then tightened again as the bucket filled up.

He gave a huff of relief. There was water.

Darren came over and helped him wind it up again.

"Come over and have a drink, Mim." Charlie spoke gently to show he was no longer angry.

She was too hot and thirsty to do anything but come. She knelt down by the bucket, and drank from cupped hands. Then the boys drank.

"Can we have something to eat?" Darren asked. He looked to Charlie and so did Mim. At the moment, he seemed to be the only one of them who had some idea of just what was happening to them.

Charlie undid the takeaway wrapping, remembering the policeman who had stopped the skyslip to buy this for them. That policeman had seemed upset by what was happening. The other two with him had not even seemed interested.

What was it that policeman had said?

Something like, "Have a feast, kids. Make your last meal a good one."

Inside the wrapping there were three hamburgers. Three apple pie rolls. A dozen Mars Bars—Charlie almost laughed, they still had them—and three small packets of chewing gum.

He took three pieces of gum from a packet, and put everything else away.

"One piece of gum!" Mim cried. "That cop said to have a feast!"

"He also said to make our last meal a good one!" Charlie said, standing. He was angry again, and frightened. Didn't the other two understand what a good last meal meant? Hadn't they ever watched a western or a cop show? He just couldn't work out why it was such a crime to accidentally slip into somewhere through time? It shouldn't bring a death sentence.

Charlie walked away from the well. Passing from the shade of the date palms into the open desert, he staggered from the heat. Even in the last few minutes, the sun seemed to have got even hotter. It struck down on his skull with painful force.

He went on for several paces, thinking he would just walk, and walk, until he could not walk any further. But the heat that now came up through his shoes, and the heat that burned into his skull, changed his mind. He turned unsteadily, feeling weak at the knees by the time he regained the shade. He dropped to a kneeling position by the bucket and scooped water up over his head and face, letting it run in streamlets down over his shoulders and chest.

"Is it that hot?" Darren asked.

Charlie nodded, and sat back on his heels. "Open the food up," he said. "If we don't eat it all now, it's going to go bad."

Mim tore the wrapping off.

"But it's all we've got," Darren said softly. "You said it before."

Charlie shrugged, and took the hamburger Mim passed him. "We're not going to even care about eating, soon," he said.

CHAPTER FIVE

Rescue

THE LITTLE OLD skyslip shook its way across the desert sands. It was a 2090 T-Model, quite old and not often seen any more. It was covered in dents and dust. The skyslip had probably been a bright, rich yellow when it left the factory. It was difficult to tell, now.

When it was new, it had been able to fly as high as a fourteen-storey building. But that was a long time ago. Now, it rattled and shook and could only manage to stay about knee-high above the ground.

Mitch peered through the windscreen.

He was glad that at least the air conditioning was working.

Officer Tammy Hansen found nothing to her liking, not even the air conditioning. She sat, stony-faced, in the passenger seat, and glared at the heat haze that rose from the endless sands.

She did not want to be here. She did not want this duty. She was convinced the guy beside her was the worst kind of nutter. As a precaution, she checked that the control device tucked into her belt was easy to access and ready to use.

"People lived here once," Mitch said. "Nomads. Well not actually lived here, but crossed it. On camels. Caravans of them. Traders. I've heard some still do."

"Not people," Tammy said. "Ferals."

"Well … you know. Ferals are people."

Tammy just snorted. Mitch ducked his head and concentrated on the way ahead. He would not like to cross this cop.

The inboard controls screen indicated that the oasis was just a few minutes ahead. He squinted and peered forward. Perhaps those upside-down palms floating above the

horizon line were a mirage of
the real thing.

"Um, just a couple more
minutes," he said.

"They give any problems
and they'll be in trouble,"
Tammy muttered feeling for
her control device, again.

"They're in trouble
anyway," Mitch said. "I just
want them left alive long
enough to make some notes."
He decided to reinforce the
words, and pulled the official form from his
wallet and began to unfold it.

"Put it away," she said. "I wouldn't be
here if I didn't know you had it."

They closed quickly on the oasis. The
T-Models had been soundless when they
were first built, but time had changed that.
There was enough noise from this one to
alert the three children. From the skyslip,
Mitch and Tammy saw them stand quickly,
pointing...

"Hide!" Mim cried. But the boys just
remained motionless, watching.

There was nowhere to hide, except the well, and none of them wanted to jump into that hole of darkness. They could already see the two people inside the skyslip, so it was certain they had been seen.

"Pretend we're lost," Darren said, looking to Charlie.

Charlie shrugged, but Mim grasped the chance.

"Yes. We're lost and we need help," she said. "They won't just leave us here. Ordinary people wouldn't do that."

"One of them's a cop," Charlie said. "Don't forget who left us here."

"They don't know that," Mim tried. But she did not seem convinced, and just stood, watching.

The skyslip settled in the sand under the shade of the palms, and the doors slid back.

"It's Mitch," Charlie said in surprise.

"Hello there," Mitch called. He rubbed his head self-consciously. "Um…we met, er, yesterday."

"We remember you," Darren assured him. "You told us about the park having once been a hospital."

"Yes," Mitch responded, forgetting the um which usually prefaced everything he said. "That meant something to you, didn't it?" He was excited, now. "You're not, um…ferals, are you?"

"No, we are not!" Mim almost shouted. "We're just lost in time because stupid Darren," she gave him a ferocious look, "is always experimenting with things!"

"That's my maths," Mitch cried, forgetting the um again. "The kind of maths I do! Testing theories of space and time. I could, um…perhaps learn something from you."

"They're ferals!" Tammy sneered. This guy is a real geek, she thought.

"We've jumped a hundred and twenty years in time!" Darren said, still barely able to believe it.

"Can you help us get back?" Mim asked Mitch, totally ignoring Tammy. "Please?"

"One hundred and, um…twenty years?" Mitch asked, a whistle of amazement in his voice. "Well…um…I can try." He was very excited, now, and climbed out of the skyslip, blinking in momentary distress as the full heat of the desert struck him.

"I've got this temporary release." He patted all of his pockets, found his wallet and took it out.

"Release?" Mim asked.

"Five days," Mitch said. "Um...yes." He unfolded the permit. "If you, er, wouldn't mind coming back with me."

"We'll come, anywhere!" they all said, almost together.

"There are a few rules, first," Tammy said as she, too, climbed out.

"We don't mind rules," Darren said.

"You don't have a choice," Tammy said, and took three narrow bracelets from a leather pouch. "Right arms, out!"

Mim and Charlie snapped their right arms out. Darren, who never had worked out his left from his right, snapped his left arm out. Then he checked with the others and changed arms just as the police officer was going to shout at him.

She stepped forward and clipped a thin metal bracelet about the wrist of each of them, and stepped back.

"Ten paces forward, run," she shouted.

The three children jerked forward. But they had only gone a pace or two before they contorted and fell screaming to the ground.

"You, um…did not need to do that," Mitch said angrily.

"Do you want to take them back, or not?" Tammy snapped.

Mitch put his hands into his pockets and stamped away, leaving Tammy with the three children. They lay, sobbing on the ground, their bodies still twitching.

"That was a warning," Tammy said. "That was only a jolt. If you take one step without my orders, you get a full snap. On your feet."

Somehow, they did get back onto their feet. Tammy directed them into the rear seat of the skyslip and took her seat in front. But it was some minutes before Mitch could regain control of his emotions and get back in behind the controls.

"Wormholes," Mitch said when they had been travelling for a while. The children were still shaking. Somehow he had to calm them. Get their trust.

"Funny little squiggly things that go right through time. Albert Einstein worked them out." He had a sudden flash of amazement. "He worked them out before you were born!"

"I've heard his name," Darren managed, his voice dull. He felt he had to speak before he was ordered to by the police officer, frightened she would reinforce her order with some force.

"Um…genius," Mitch said, wondering what he could say next.

The T-Model was flying even lower than it had been on the way out. The weight of an extra three people was really testing the old bucket.

"Why did you come to get us?" Mim asked. "I mean, just for five days."

"To study you," he said.

"Study us?" Mim asked. She was about to say more when she noted a flicker of annoyance cross the police officer's face. She shivered, and was quiet.

Mitch caught her feeling of fear, and spoke again quickly. "To help you, now that I understand what happened. If you know it can be done, then, um…it can be done!"

Charlie was moving about, checking the seat on each side of him.

"I can't find a seat belt," he mumbled.

"Seat belt?" Mitch asked, puzzled. His eyes blinked and he looked about.

"In case of an accident," Charlie said, keeping a wary eye on the police officer. "So we won't get thrown around or anything."

"Ah!" Mitch exclaimed, delighted to have a topic of conversation. "Don't use them. Force fields now. If there is a sudden stop or bump you will only move a very little bit. Just enough to cushion you. It's science."

"That's what the police must have used when they were taking us in," Charlie said. "Except they had it switched on all the time so we couldn't even move."

"Exactly," Mitch agreed. "Do you think you're in the same world?"

They were puzzled. "I mean, you've slipped through time. What about space?"

"I think so," Darren said. "That it's still the same world. Just one hundred and twenty years later."

"Can't you... can't you just send us home?" Mim whispered.

"Two ends," Mitch said. "Wormholes have two ends. If you could pop out one end, you should be able to pop right back in again." He blinked his eyes and shook his head, almost sad.

"Um... trick is to find the slippery little things."

The T-Model left the desert and moved into green country; then stopped at an entry to a main road.

"Have to put the wheels down here," Mitch explained.

"Then I just lock into home and All Roads Control takes over. And what were you doing?"

They looked at him, not having a clue what his question was about.

"Um, when you slipped…um, slipped through. What were you actually doing?"

"Playing with his stupid crystal set," Mim said, looking at Darren.

"It's a kind of radio without a battery," Darren explained. "I don't think any of this would have happened if Mim hadn't said we should try a different crystal. It was a crystal we found on an excursion."

"They have a display," Mitch said. "At the museum." He changed something on the computer. "I'll show you." He blinked and rubbed his hair. "Um…yes…I'll show you."

CHAPTER SIX

The Crystal Set

EVERYONE AT THE museum seemed to know him and did not seem at all surprised to see him with a cop and three very strange children.

Mitch knew children well. Before he took them near any displays, he led them into a cafeteria and fed them. Tammy refused to take part, but Mitch ate heaps, they noticed, wondering why he was so skinny.

The display of old radios was in a basement room that was not open to the public. It was a display that was not well cared for, and Charlie backed away when he saw cobwebs.

He was not afraid of much, but spiders gave him the creeps.

Tammy took a place by the door, and they realised she was watching every move they made. They each fingered the bracelets on their wrists, feeling a sickening sensation as the vivid memory of what they could do re-entered their minds.

But she did not appear to want to control their every move.

Mim and Charlie followed Mitch as he led them around the display. It was not until they turned to go into another aisle that they realised Darren was not with them.

They spun round, their eyes looking wildly about until they found Tammy. She had not moved from her station by the door; so it was nothing she had done.

"Darren!" Charlie shouted, ignoring the frowns of disapproval of the few people around. He shouted the name again. "Darren. Where are you?"

"There," Mim cried.

Darren was standing with his eyes fixed on a part of the display. They ran back to him, so relieved that for a brief moment they even forgot about Tammy and her power to control them.

"Look at this," whispered Darren, pointing with his finger. "See, it's mine. That's the crystal set I built."

Mim moved to look at it, closely. "How could it be? But it is," she said, shocked.

Charlie peered at it from behind. He was not going near anything with spider webs on it.

Mitch had followed them. He looked where they were looking, then blinked several times and rubbed his head with one hand. He was trying to understand what they were saying.

Mim turned to him. "This is the crystal set Darren was using when we were snatched."

"But not with a normal crystal in it," Darren continued. "We found this crystal when we were on an excursion with Mr Johns, our teacher, and Mim said we should try it in the crystal set."

"Mr Johns thought it might have been part of a meteor," Charlie added.

"And you put it in and…and, pow you were here?" Mitch asked.

"No. It didn't seem to work, so I went out to check the aerial," Darren said.

"Well…why don't we set it up here and see what happens?" Mitch suggested. He looked along the room. "There's plenty of space to do it."

"Why don't we set it up in the park where we landed? Then everything will be the same. It will make it a real experiment," Mim said. She had some idea that, once they were out in the park, they might have a chance to get home.

Mitch blinked, and pointed a finger at her. "You," he cried, "are brilliant. What do we need? I'll have some of my students come and help."

When they got to the university, they were relieved to find they did not have to squeeze a lot of students into the T-Model for the trip to the park. They travelled in a university skyslip. When they arrived, Darren headed straight for the fountain.

"Here's the mark we made when we landed," Darren said, finding the two lines that he and Charlie had hacked into the lawn with the heels of their shoes. "If we were home on my lawn, this spot would be the middle of the aerial wire."

Mitch gave some instructions to his students. They set up the two tall tripods which they had brought with them to hold the aerial wire.

"Now what?" Mitch asked.

Darren attached the wire to the crystal set. Then he put the earpiece in and listened. "It's making exactly the same noises as it did at home," he said, surprised. He handed the earpiece to Mitch.

"Interesting," Mitch said. "Then what happened?"

"I went out onto the lawn to look at the aerial," Darren said. He began to walk towards the place under the aerial, then stopped and looked at the bracelet on his wrist. "I wasn't wearing this, though."

"Well, you're wearing it now," Tammy snapped.

"It might not be the same," Darren said,

walking on. "Something happened that was very strange. Anything could change it."

"Um…do you think he could have it off, just for the experiment?" Mitch asked Tammy. "You won't try to bolt, will you?" he asked Darren anxiously.

"He won't live if he does," Tammy said. She checked her control device, then took the bracelet off.

"Um…we were in that experiment, too," Mim said. She held her arm hesitantly towards Tammy.

"I hope you know what you are doing," Tammy said to Mitch as she took the bracelet from Mim's arm.

"Well, no, not really," Mitch admitted. "That's the thing with experiments. You never do know until it's done. But, I do know that to duplicate an experiment, um, everything has to be exactly the same as it was the first time."

"Except the year, I hope," Darren said under his breath, a sudden sense of excitement gripping him.

Tammy gave Mitch a look that said he was an idiot, then took the bracelet from

Charlie's arm as well, and rested her hand on the butt of her control device.

"Um … so?" Mitch looked at Darren.

"Well I walked out to here, below the middle of the aerial," Darren said, taking up his position below the wire.

"Then he began to go invisible, so we ran out to see what was wrong," Mim said.

Mitch blinked several times. "I think he's doing that now," Mitch said, then made urgent motions of his hand for her to run out. "Quick. Um … hurry."

Mim glanced nervously at Tammy, then ran, and Charlie ran with her.

"Look, he is going invisible again!" Mim whispered.

"Pretend to pull him away!" Charlie said. "But just pretend! We might be going home!"

They both snatched hold of Darren, and looked back to the others. There was something different happening now. Or, perhaps not different. It may just have been that there was nothing moving when they had been on Darren's back lawn. Now Mitch, the students, and Tammy all seemed to be moving in slow motion.

The control device Tammy was pulling from her belt, came out in slow motion.

The children clutched each other. They saw Mitch begin a slow-motion leap towards Tammy and knew he was going to knock the device from her hand. But even as they realised that, they knew that he would not reach her in time.

The control device in Tammy's hand jolted. A beam streamed from the end of it. Then, a hand's stretch from them, the beam seemed to split. It became a wall of streaming fire as though it had splattered against an invisible barrier. Then there was just white light. If they had not been through this before, they would have thought they had been hit.

It was just like their first journey, even the lawn under their feet was gone.

They were standing on nothing, yet did not seem to be falling. It was more like floating. No, it wasn't even like that. If they had been floating, they would have been moving, even if it was just a little bit.

"Faster than light…"

The voice came like an echo from the past, and then they were standing on grass again. It was the grass in the back yard of Darren's house. And they could move. They had made it back again.

Mim took one look around and bolted. "Trash that stupid crystal set before it gets you again!" she screamed back just before she disappeared down beside the house.

Darren nodded dumbly. "I will," he said.

"No!" Charlie said urgently. "Just take some wires off. You've got to give the crystal set to the museum, or it will not be there when we need it."

"But we're back," Darren said, as he opened the door of the house.

"We only got back because the crystal set was there," Charlie said. "If you trash it now, we'll be stuck in the year 2120. Can't you see that? Even Mitch can't find wormholes yet.

You have to make sure the crystal set is in the museum before you die. Even if we have to make a donation or something, it has to be there. Otherwise we won't be able to come back. Do you understand?"

Darren stopped in the kitchen and tried to work out what Charlie was saying, but it made no sense to him.

"Do you see?" Charlie said again.

"Nuh," Darren admitted. "But I'll do what you said, anyway."

"And when you're grown up you have to leave that message on the telephone."

"What?" Darren asked.

"The message you got in the cellcom," Charlie said. "When Mitch gave us the tokens." He was becoming angry. "You've got to promise me!"

Slowly Darren began to make sense of what Charlie was saying. They had travelled through time. They had come back because the same crystal set that had sent them was there in the museum, one hundred and twenty years on, to send them back again.

"Yes," Darren said, suddenly beginning to understand. "I do see what you mean."

"Now, I have to go home." Charlie glanced at the kitchen clock. "It's almost time for me to get dinner ready for my mother and father."

"We haven't been away for very long, have we," Darren said.

"No," Charlie said. "I don't think time has passed. We just passed through time."

Darren nodded slowly. He was still nodding when he reached his room. But it did not mean he understood.

The first thing he did was to take the aerial wire off the crystal set. Then he packed the set into a shoe box. When his father came home, Darren got him to help take down the aerial. He wound that up in loops, and put it into the shoe box, too. Then he put the shoe box into a drawer.

He did not have to give it to the museum straight away. It would probably be easier to persuade them to take it when he was older. He knew he was going to live until he was quite old. The recording in the cellcom had told him that.

Darren heard the back door close and went out to the kitchen. His mother had arrived home and was helping his father make dinner.

"Have a good day?" she asked.

He nodded, and took a piece of carrot to chew on. "It was a bit weird, though," he said as he left to turn on the TV.

Darren did not really feel normal again until the next morning when he was getting his school lunch. His mum and dad had put two chocolate bars in for him—they often did things like that. This is how things are supposed to be, he thought, taking a bite from one before he packed them.

He had been thinking about yesterday a lot since he woke up. The more he thought about it, the more he realised nothing like that could ever really happen. Except in a dream. He laughed. Hadn't Mim kept saying that, even while they were in the dream?

He sighed with relief. Who wanted to know the future? And who could, anyway?

He would tell Mim and Charlie about his dream when he got to school. And he could use it as an essay, too.

Darren put his lunch into his school bag and went out the door. He was feeling great.

But he never wanted to have another dream like that again. That dream had felt too real for comfort!

And then he stopped dead, and just gaped.

In the middle of the back lawn, eyes blinking in confusion, one hand rubbing his head in puzzlement, stood Mitch…